DATE DUE

NOV 2 4 1998	
MAR 0 7 2000	
OCT 1 4 2000	
OCT 2 7 2000	
OCT 1 4 2010	

The Library Store   #47-0107

✍ PROFILES OF GREAT ✍
BLACK AMERICANS

Female Leaders

✍✍

Edited by Richard Rennert
Introduction by Coretta Scott King

Ill A Chelsea House
Ill Multibiography

Chelsea House Publishers
New York   Philadelphia

On the cover: Rosa Parks at the time of the Montgomery bus boycott.

Copyright © 1994 by Chelsea House Publishers, a division of Main Line Book Co. All rights reserved. Printed and bound in the United States of America.

5 7 9 8 6 4 2

Library of Congress Cataloging-in-Publication Data

Female Leaders/edited by Richard Rennert.
p. cm.—(Profiles of great Black Americans)
(A Chelsea House multibiography)
Includes bibliographical references and index.
Contents: Shirley Chisholm—Marian Wright Edelman—
Barbara Jordan—Coretta Scott King—Carol Moseley-Braun—
Rosa Parks—Madam C. J. Walker—Ida Wells-Barnett.
ISBN   0-7910-2057-6.
        0-7910-2058-4 (pbk.)
    1. Afro-American women—Biography—Juvenile literature.
[1. Women—Biography. 2. Afro-Americans—Biography.]
I. Rennert, Richard. II. Series. III. Series: A Chelsea House
multibiography
E185.96.F46 1993   93-16425
920.72'08996073—dc20   CIP
[B]   AC

✺ CONTENTS ✺

❧ INTRODUCTION ❧

by Coretta Scott King

This book is about black Americans who served society through the excellence of their achievements. It forms a part of the rich history of black men and women in America—a history of stunning accomplishments in every field of human endeavor, from literature and art to science, industry, education, diplomacy, athletics, jurisprudence, even polar exploration.

Not all of the people in this history had the same ideals, but I think you will find something that all of them had in common. Like Martin Luther King, Jr., they all decided to become "drum majors" and serve humanity. In that principle—whether it was expressed in books, inventions, or song—they found something outside themselves to use as a goal and a guide. Something that showed them a way to serve others instead of only living for themselves.

Reading the stories of these courageous men and women not only helps us discover the principles that we will use to guide our own lives but also teaches us about our black heritage and about America itself. It is crucial for us to know the heroes and heroines of our history and to realize that the price we paid in our struggle for equality in America was dear. But we must also understand that we have gotten as far as we have partly because America's democratic system and ideals made it possible.

We are still struggling with racism and prejudice. But the great men and women in this series are a tribute to the spirit of our democratic ideals and the system in which they have flourished. And that makes their stories special and worth knowing.

SHIRLEY CHISHOLM

Shirley Chisholm, America's first black congresswoman, was born Shirley Anita St. Hill on November 20, 1924, in the Bedford-Stuyvesant section of Brooklyn, New York. She was the oldest of Ruby and Charles St. Hill's four daughters. Hoping to save money for the girls' education, their parents sent them to live with their grandmother in Barbados in 1927. Seven years later, Shirley and her sisters returned to the United States, which was by then in the grip of the Great Depression.

Like millions of other Americans of the 1930s, the St. Hills had very little money, but they never considered letting a school-age child work. To Charles St. Hill, a fifth-grade dropout himself, education came first. His girls rewarded his faith by doing well at school; Shirley led the pack by graduating at the top of her high school class and receiving scholarship offers from Vassar and Oberlin. Unable to afford a distant school even on a scholarship, Shirley St. Hill enrolled in Brooklyn College, from which she graduated cum laude in 1946.

Urged by her college professors to consider politics as a career, star pupil St. Hill had demurred: "You forget two things," she said. "I'm black—and I'm a woman." After college, she took a job at a Harlem child-care center, where she worked for seven years while studying for a master's degree in early childhood education at Columbia University night school. She received the degree in 1952. During this period, she met and married a recent immigrant from Jamaica, graduate student Conrad Chisholm.

From 1953 to 1964, Shirley Chisholm served as an educational consultant for the New York City Bureau of Child Welfare. Meanwhile, she had finally entered politics. In 1960, the 36-year-old educator, along with a group of reform-minded neighbors, decided to oust the local Democratic political machine and replace it with a new, liberal party organization. Their group, the Unity Democratic Club, failed in its first bid to take over the district, but their second try, in 1962, fared differently.

That year, the Unity Club managed to place two of its candidates on the slate. Both won election to the New York State Assembly, thereby giving control of the 17th Assembly District to the reformers. Two years later, one of these assemblymen became a judge, leaving a vacant slot. Chisholm decided to fill it herself.

After what she later called "a long, hard summer and fall," Shirley Chisholm swept to a win in a three-way contest, racking up 18,151 votes to her nearest opponent's 1,893. She went to Albany, New York's capital, and from 1964 until 1968 served as assemblywoman for the 17th District. During those four years, the Brooklyn woman proved herself a tough, independent politician. Among her accomplishments was the enactment into law of two of her pet projects: SEEK, a program providing college funds for poor youngsters, and an unemployment insurance fund for domestic employees.

After two terms in Albany, Assemblywoman Chisholm turned her eyes toward the nation's capital. A redistricting of her residential area created the new, predominantly black 12th Congressional District. Nominated by an independent citizens' committee, she defeated the party regular for the nomination, then went on to defeat the Republican candidate, Congress of Racial Equality founder James Farmer.

In early 1969, Congresswoman Shirley Chisholm took her seat in the House of Representatives—the first black woman ever to do so.

As a member of the 91st Congress, Chisholm showed herself as independent minded as she had been in the state legislature. When House leaders assigned her to the Agricultural Committee—a post they had assumed she would appreciate because of the committee's jurisdiction over food stamps—Chisholm astonished her colleagues by protesting vehemently. Showing unusual political skill for a congressional freshman, she managed to get herself reassigned, first to the Veterans Affairs Committee, where she served two years, then to her first choice: the powerful Education and Labor Committee. Demonstrating her sentiments—and her strengths—Chisholm helped engineer passage of a number of major bills. Included were laws that aided the poor, increased minimum wages, and created federal subsidies to support day-care centers for working mothers.

In 1970, voters of the 12th Congressional District enthusiastically returned Chisholm to Washington. But as a congresswoman, she soon felt she had pushed her agenda as far as possible. To accomplish what she believed America needed—among other things, a more equitable share of work and power for minorities and women—she decided to aim for the top. In 1972, she announced her candidacy for the Democratic nomination for president of the United States. Never before in the nation's history had a

black or a woman—to say nothing of a *black woman*—
sought the presidential nomination of a major party.

Chisholm had acquired a core of dedicated campaign workers and supporters, but with limited funds
at their disposal, these loyalists made scant headway
against the well-financed, well-organized opposition.
When Chisholm went to the Democratic National
Convention in 1972, she went with only 24 committed
delegates. Candidate Hubert Humphrey, aware that
he could not block the candidacy of South Dakota's
senator George McGovern, released his delegates to
Chisholm, but the battle was not even close. Mc-
Govern took the nomination, going on to lose the
election (by a landslide) to incumbent Richard Nixon.

Despite her failure to capture the presidential
nomination, Chisholm looked on the effort as its own
kind of triumph. She spoke to reporters after the
election:

> In terms of black politics, I think an effect of my campaign
> has been to increase the independence and self-reliance of
> many local elected black officials and black political activists
> from the domination of the political "superstars." The United
> States was said not to be ready to elect a Catholic to the
> presidency when Al Smith [Governor Alfred E. Smith of New
> York, a Democrat and a Roman Catholic, who lost to
> Republican Herbert Hoover in 1928] ran in the 1920s. But
> Smith's nomination may have helped pave the way for the
> successful campaign John F. Kennedy [a Roman Catholic
> Massachusetts senator] waged in 1960. Who can tell? What I
> hope most is that now there will be others who will feel

themselves as capable of running for high political office as any wealthy, good-looking white male.

Undiscouraged by her unsuccessful tilt at the presidency, Chisholm sought and easily won reelection to Congress in 1972. By this time, she had gained a secure national reputation for her undeviating advocacy of minority and women's rights. She once said that although she had been the first black woman elected to the U.S. Congress, she wanted to be remembered instead "as a catalyst for change, a woman who had the determination and a woman who had the perseverance to fight on behalf of the female population and the black population, because I'm a product of both."

As the years passed—Chisholm would eventually win and serve a total of seven terms in Congress—the Brooklyn maverick came somewhat closer to joining ranks with the party she represented. But she still resisted party discipline, sticking to her own route when she saw it as best for her constituents. She voted, for example, against several Democratic-backed bills that aimed at protecting the environment, asserting that their immediate result would be job losses among the poor.

In February 1982, Chisholm announced her retirement; she would finish out her term, but she would not be a candidate in November 1982. Supporters reacted with dismay, but many understood that personal reasons played a large role in the congresswoman's decision. In 1977, soon after a quiet divorce from Conrad Chisholm, 52-year-old Shirley Chisholm married Arthur Hardwick, Jr., a black businessman and former New York State assemblyman. Two years after the wedding, Hardwick had almost died in an automobile accident; Chisholm found the conflict between caring for her recovering husband and serving in Congress more than she wished to face. As one observer put it, "Her husband's accident and the new conservative climate in Washington [rightwing Republican Ronald Reagan had been elected in 1980] prompted Shirley to think about her own goals."

After retiring from politics, Chisholm taught political science and women's studies at Mount Holyoke College; she also gave frequent lectures and, in 1985, accepted the post of honorary scholar at Spelman College. Her husband died in 1986, and she gave up her teaching positions shortly afterward. In 1988, she joined Jesse Jackson's campaign for the presidency, just as she had four years earlier.

In the mid-1980s, Chisholm created a new organization, the National Political Caucus of Black Women, which soon counted thousands of members across the United States. An active member of the League of Women Voters, the National Association for the Advancement of Colored People, and the National Board of Americans for Democratic Action, she has also written two autobiographies: *Unbought and Unbossed* and *The Good Fight*.

MARIAN WRIGHT EDELMAN

$\mathbf{M}$arian Wright Edelman, founding president of the Children's Defense Fund (CDF), was born Marian Wright on June 6, 1939, in Bennettsville, South Carolina. Named for groundbreaking black contralto Marian Anderson, she was the youngest of five children born to clergyman Arthur Jerome Wright and his activist wife, Maggie

Bowen Wright. Arthur Wright, a disciple of educator Booker T. Washington, set high standards for his children: they must not only obtain the best possible education, he said, they must use it to help others. "Working for the community," recalled the adult Marian Wright, "was as much a part of our existence as eating and sleeping and church."

Both Maggie Wright, who operated a home for the elderly in Bennettsville, and her husband, pastor of the town's Shiloh Baptist Church, exerted a strong influence on their youngest daughter. Arthur Wright died in 1954, but Maggie Wright carried on his ideals; when Marian graduated from high school, her mother sent her to Spelman College, a black liberal arts school in Atlanta, Georgia. There Marian racked up such an outstanding record that she won a fellowship to study in Europe during her junior year.

Wright attended the Sorbonne in Paris for one semester, the University of Geneva in Switzerland for another, then spent the summer studying the work of Russian writer Leo Tolstoy in the Soviet Union. After 15 months abroad she returned home in the fall of 1959—and experienced something of a shock. Europeans had seemed virtually color-blind, but in Wright's own country, segregation's grip remained tight, especially in her native South.

As it happened, Wright's return to the United States coincided with the dawn of the 1960s—a decade of antidiscrimination protests that would rock the South and eventually outlaw segregation. In Wright's senior year at Spelman, she took part in a student sit-in at Atlanta's city hall and wound up in the city jail. The arrest triggered a major switch in her career plans: Instead of getting a graduate degree in Russian studies, then entering the nation's diplomatic corps, Wright now decided to go to law school and specialize in civil rights law. A crusader had been born.

Wright graduated from Spelman—as valedictorian of her class—in 1960. That year, she explained her new motives in an article in the college newspaper:

> I realize that I am not fighting just for myself and my people in the South when I fight for freedom and equality. I realize now that I fight for the moral and political health of America as a whole and for her position in the world at large. . . . I know that I, in my individual struggle for improvement, help the world. I am no longer an isolated being—I belong.

Not only accepted by prestigious Yale University Law School but given a scholarship, Wright headed for New Haven, Connecticut, in the fall of 1960. In her last year of law school, she reached another of her life decisions, this one sparked by a visit to Mississippi. After spending spring break helping the Student Nonviolent Coordinating Committee (SNCC) with a voter-registration drive, she vowed that as soon as she received her law degree, she would return to the South and work for civil rights, preferably under the banner of the National Association for the Advancement of Colored People (NAACP).

Those who knew Marian Wright had long understood one essential feature of her personality: what she said she would do, she would do. After graduating from Yale in 1963, she spent a year training in New York City, then went to work as a legal intern with the NAACP Legal Defense and Education Fund in Jackson, Mississippi. Inspiring Wright—who was one of the Legal Defense Fund's first two interns—was the daring and charismatic Thurgood Marshall. The NAACP attorney, who would later become the nation's first black Supreme Court justice, had headed the Defense Fund since 1938. In the 1960s, he spearheaded the NAACP's campaign to wipe out segregation and racism.

Marshall was unswerving in his support for the right to protest, a right by no means taken for granted in the mid–20th-century American South. "Protest is part of our tradition," he said. "It goes back to tea dumped in Boston Harbor. [Blacks] have a right to say they want their rights."

Marian Wright agreed wholeheartedly. In Mississippi, she spent much of her time arranging for the release of protesting students from illegal detention. No more popular with white southern lawmen than was Marshall himself, Wright sometimes wound up in jail along with her clients. Although she was an accredited lawyer, she also found herself refused entry into certain courthouses as well as threatened by snarling police dogs. Did she, someone once asked her at the time, ever doubt the ability of the law to change southern segregationist ways? "Sure, like every morning," she shot back. "But one keeps plugging, trying to make our institutional processes work."

In 1964, the 25-year-old South Carolinian became head of the NAACP Legal Defense Fund in Mississippi, a position she would hold for the next four years. In 1965, she became the first black woman to pass the bar (obtain the right to practice law) in Mississippi. But even as she crusaded tirelessly for civil rights, Wright began to realize that before the situation changed in Mississippi, it would have to change in the nation's capital. Accordingly, she applied for and received a grant from the Field Foundation and, in 1968, moved to Washington, D.C., and established the Washington Research Project, predecessor of the Children's Defense Fund. "It became clear to me that the poor needed a voice in Washington, just like General Motors and other big interests have," she told an interviewer in 1993.

In Washington, D.C., Wright reencountered Peter Edelman, a white fellow civil rights worker she had met in Mississippi. In July 1968, four months after her move to the capital, Wright married Edelman. The couple worked in Washington until 1971, when they both accepted new jobs in Boston, Massachusetts. Marian Wright Edelman became director of the Harvard University Center for Law and Education, a position she held while making twice-weekly flights back to Washington to oversee the Research Project—and while raising her two sons, Joshua and Jonah. (A third son, Ezra, was born to the couple in 1974.)

In 1973, Marian Edelman founded the Children's Defense Fund (CDF), a Washington-based organization that aimed at providing long-range assistance to children and at getting children's issues included in public policy. Six years later, Edelman and her husband returned to the nation's capital, he to teach at the Georgetown University Law Center, she to concentrate on the CDF.

In the years since then, Marian Wright Edelman has dedicated herself to the young, earning herself a national nickname: "the children's crusader." She has zeroed in on a diverse range of related topics, starting with teenage pregnancy. "I saw from our own statistics that 55 $\frac{1}{2}$ percent of all black babies were born out of wedlock, a great many to teenage girls," she told a reporter in 1983. "It just hit me over the head," she continued, "that that situation ensured black child poverty for the next generation."

Under Edelman's direction, the CDF staged a massive campaign to help prevent unwanted pregnancies among black teenagers. Offering options to pregnancy, CDF messages appeared in buses and subways, on radio and television broadcasts, and on posters in teen gathering places. And in late 1987, the U.S. Senate passed the Act for Better Child Care, legislation designed and sponsored by Edelman's CDF.

As Edelman sees it, the CDF's mission is vast but simple: to improve the lot of America's children. The organization aims to teach the general population about children's needs and to encourage investment in preventive rather than remedial care. In other words, the Fund wants to help children before they become mentally, physically, or emotionally ill, drop out of school, get pregnant, or run afoul of the law. The CDF also concerns itself with young people's employment.

Dynamically energetic, Edelman serves on many boards, including those of the Yale University Corporation, the Carnegie Council on Children, Spelman College, the NAACP, Citizens for Constitutional Concerns, the Joint Center for Political Studies, the U.S. Committee for UNICEF, the Center for Budget and Policy Priorities, and the March of Dimes. She is also a member of the Council on Foreign Relations. In 1985 she became a MacArthur Foundation Prize Fellow.

Among Edelman's many publications are *Children out of School in America*; *Families in Peril: An Agenda for Social Change*; *Portrait of Inequality: Black and White Children in America*; and, in 1992, the best-selling *The Measure of Our Success: A Letter to My Children and Yours*.

BARBARA JORDAN

Barbara Charlene Jordan, the South's first black U.S. congresswoman, was born in 1936 in a poor black neighborhood of Houston, Texas. She grew up in a small two-bedroom house shared with her parents, Arlyne and Benjamin, her two older sisters, and her grandparents.

Barbara bristled at the rules laid down by her father, warehouse clerk and preacher Benjamin Jordan: no movies, no novels or comic books, no card playing, no dancing, and church all day on Sunday. He also demanded that his daughters gain a first-rate education. ("No man," he told them, "can take away your brain.") With that, however, Barbara had no problem: she sailed through school with a virtually straight-A average.

In high school, Barbara became a formidable debater. By the time she graduated, she had been named "Girl of the Year" by her classmates and had collected more than a dozen medals for "Declamation" and "Outstanding Accomplishments in Speech." Barbara Jordan enrolled in Texas Southern University (TSU), a new, all-black Houston college, in 1952. In college, she continued her triumphal record as a debater. Her voice was commanding and deep, her vocabulary extensive, her wit quick and sometimes biting. "She had a truly God-given talent for speaking," commented one impressed rival.

Soon acknowledged as the university's star debater, Jordan traveled with the TSU debating team, meeting and crushing opposing teams in cities as far off as Chicago, Boston, and New York. Jordan and her friends enjoyed the contests, but their carefree days were darkened by racial discrimination and segregation, then facts of American life. "You had to plan for food and even plan ahead to locate service stations where blacks could use restrooms," recalled one of Jordan's teammates.

In 1954, attorney Thurgood Marshall of the National Association for the Advancement of Colored

People won a spectacular Supreme Court victory—
the school-segregation challenge known as *Brown v.
Board of Education of Topeka*—that began the slow but
eventual desegregation of the nation's public schools
and other public places. Jordan had already been
thinking of law as a career; after Marshall's triumph,
she made up her mind to do it. Graduating from TSU
with honors in 1956, she entered Boston University
Law School. She received her law degree in 1959, then
headed back to Houston, where she opened a law
office in her family's dining room.

Not very busy at first, Jordan decided to try political volunteerism. As a county Democratic Committee
aide, she helped round up voters for the ticket headed
by John F. Kennedy and Texan Lyndon B. Johnson.
The Democrats won, and Jordan made an important
self-discovery: "I had really been bitten," she said
later, "by the political bug."

The 24-year-old lawyer also discovered that her
debater's skills translated handily to the political
stump. In 1961, she became president of the Harris
County Democrats, joined the Houston Council on
Human Relations, and won the presidency of the
all-black, hitherto all-male Houston Lawyers Association. The following year, she ran for a seat in the
Texas House of Representatives. Defeated by a white
male candidate, Jordan received some harsh advice
from a local political expert.

"You're black, you're a woman, and you're large,"
said the pundit, adding, "People don't really like that
image." He recommended that she drop politics.

Characteristically, Jordan listened, then went her own way. In 1964, she ran again—and lost again. "I did not like losing," she said. In 1965, she ran for state senator. After a grueling contest with another white male opponent, she won the election by a margin of two to one. In January 1967, she became Texas's first black state senator since 1883.

Jordan's carefully prepared Senate speeches soon earned respect not only from her colleagues but from the president of the United States. A month into her term, President Lyndon B. Johnson invited her to Washington, D.C., to discuss a fair-housing bill, and over the next two years he invited her back several times and even appointed her to a special economics commission.

In 1968, Jordan easily won a second term in the Texas Senate. Over the next few years, she orchestrated a substantial amount of legislation, including bills dealing with workmen's compensation, unemployment, equal rights for women, low-cost housing, and the establishment of a state department of labor. In October 1971, she began raising funds for another campaign. A newly formed congressional district, established because of a shift in Texas's population, called for a new U.S. representative, and Jordan intended to be it.

Up against a hard-fighting state representative (yet another white male), Jordan now fought the political battle of her life. Among those who aided her was her friend Lyndon Johnson, by then no longer president but still awesomely powerful. (Republican Richard

Nixon had been elected president in 1968.) In May 1972, 80 percent of the 18th Congressional District's voters cast their ballots for Barbara Jordan. On January 3, 1973, the 36-year-old Texan, the first black women ever sent to the House by a southern state, took her seat in the 93rd Congress of the United States. She was soon appointed, at Johnson's suggestion, to the influential House Judiciary Committee.

From the beginning of Jordan's term, Washington had been in a state of turmoil about the Watergate scandal. It had begun in June 1972, when District of Columbia police arrested five men for breaking into Democratic National Committee offices in the Watergate building. Members of President Nixon's reelection committee, the men had been trying to discover how much the Democrats knew about Republican campaign funds. The illegal break-in triggered an avalanche that would rock the nation.

By the fall of 1973, the rumblings had begun. Nixon denied all knowledge of the Watergate break-in, but he did his best—which included a White House–directed cover-up—to cripple the congressional investigation into the episode. At this point, outraged House members introduced articles of impeachment (grounds for a trial that could lead to the president's removal from office). The articles were turned over to the House Judiciary Committee for study.

Jordan, who had an almost mystical faith in constitutional government, found the idea of impeaching the president horrifying. Nevertheless, Nixon's continued stonewalling of the issue at last led her to believe that the country's interest demanded the impeachment, and she explained her views to the American people on national television. Her meticulously reasoned, passionately delivered speech scored a bull's-eye on America's moral compass. After the address, thousands of Americans contacted Jordan's office to praise her speech and her stand. Two weeks after the speech, Nixon escaped the prospect of impeachment by resigning.

At the Democratic presidential convention two years later, Jordan made another speech that electrified the nation. Delivered from Manhattan's Madison Square Garden, her keynote address transfixed millions of Americans and helped elect Democrat Jimmy Carter. "The Democratic Party," observed the *Washington Post* the next day, "never had an opening night like this before, and never will again."

Jordan, who had been reelected to the House in a 1974 landslide, continued her frantic schedule in Washington. To the Judiciary Committee, she added membership in the House Government Operations Committee and the Steering and Policy Committee of the House Democratic Caucus, to which she was the first black women ever assigned. As a legislator, Jordan displayed a careful impartiality; although she felt an intense interest in laws that would further the rights and interests of blacks and women, she believed she had been elected to represent all the people, not just these groups. The many bills she introduced or supported in the House dealt with matters as wide ranging as crime, civil rights, fair trade laws, federal-state revenue sharing, labor, bilingual ballots, abortion, education, and the Equal Rights Amendment.

The legislator, who had been suffering since 1973 from a progressive neurological impairment (about which she refused all public comment), started using a wheelchair in the late 1970s. She never explained if her illness was what led her to leave politics, but leave she did. After six highly visible years in the House, she suddenly announced her retirement from public office in 1978, at the end of her third term.

Stating only that she needed "a new direction," Jordan left Washington and returned to Texas, where she had accepted a professorship at the University of Texas in Austin. In 1982, she was named to the Lyndon Baines Johnson Centennial Chair in National Policy at the university. From the beginning, so many students clamored to take her courses that officials awarded admission to her lectures by lottery.

Jordan has made periodic public appearances at political events such as conventions, each time demonstrating oratorical powers as awesome as ever. Most of her time, however, is spent working as an educator, a job she shows every sign of caring about intensely. Of her students, she has said, "I want them to be premier public servants who have a core of principles to guide them. They are my future, and the future of this country."

CORETTA SCOTT KING

Coretta Scott King—civil rights activist, author, lecturer, columnist, and the widow of the Reverend Martin Luther King, Jr.—was born Coretta Scott in Marion, Alabama, on April 27, 1927. One of the three children of Obadiah and Bernice Murray Scott, she graduated from Lincoln High School in Marion, then won a scholarship to Antioch College in Yellow Springs, Ohio.

The young Alabama woman had sought admission to a northern school with a purpose: she had seen enough of her native South and its whites' idea of justice toward blacks to last her a lifetime. When her father's small but promising sawmill was burned to the ground by envious whites, she made up her mind: she would leave the South and spend her life in the nonviolent world of music in the North.

A poor family, the Scotts could ill afford spending money for a daughter in college. At Antioch, from which she would earn a bachelor's degree in music and elementary education, Coretta divided her time between studying and working at a string of odd jobs. After graduation, she moved on to Boston, where she had won another scholarship, this one to study voice at the New England Conservatory of Music. To stretch her scholarship funds, Coretta cleaned her fellow students' rooms.

Studying in Boston at the same time as Coretta Scott was a divinity student from Atlanta, Georgia: Martin Luther King, Jr. The young southerner liked the North, but, he recalled telling a confidante, he missed the "particular charm" of southern women. Claiming she had the perfect solution to that problem, King's friend handed him the phone number of a student from Alabama. That night, King called Coretta Scott and asked her for a date.

"He had quite a line," recalled Coretta Scott King years afterward—but she agreed to have lunch with the smooth-talking divinity student the following day. When she met him in person, Scott saw a disappointingly short, solemn young man, but over a leisurely lunch in a Boston cafeteria, her view began to change. "The young man became increasingly better looking as he talked so strongly and convincingly," she recalled. King, meanwhile, had already decided he had met the right woman, and he told her so. "You have everything I have ever wanted in a wife," he said. "There are only four things—character, intelligence, personality, and beauty—and you have them all."

Coretta Scott had long ago made several important decisions about her life: she would leave the South, she would have a career as a singer, and she would never marry except on a basis of complete equality. King's future as a great preacher might have been predicted by his conversion of the woman he loved. She knew she wanted to marry him, but, she told him, she intended to pursue her singing career. The tradition-minded King said he would be glad to run the household until she earned her master's degree from the conservatory, but after that, he would work, and she would not. "I'm supposed to earn enough to take care of you and the family," he said.

Scott then reminded her husband-to-be that she had no intention of returning to the South. "I'm going to be pastor of a church," he replied. "I'm going to live in the South because that's where I'm needed." Somewhat to her own surprise, Scott acceded to King's wishes. "Martin was such a very strong man," she said later. In June 1953, Scott, 26, and King, 24, were married by King's father, the Reverend Martin Luther King, Sr., in the front yard of the Scotts' modest home in Marion, Alabama.

After the wedding and a summer in Atlanta, the young couple returned to Boston. There Coretta completed her requirements for a master's degree in voice, and Martin polished his doctoral dissertation (which he would complete in 1955). In late 1953, King gave a sermon at the Dexter Avenue Baptist Church in Montgomery, Alabama; soon afterward, the church offered him its pastorate. In September 1955, the Kings moved to Montgomery; there, a year later, their first child, Yolanda, was born. Her arrival would eventually be followed by those of three siblings: Martin III, born in 1957; Dexter in 1962; and Bernice in 1963.

The spring before the Kings settled in Montgomery, the Supreme Court had ruled school segregation illegal. Like Americans of all races, Coretta King saw that the black South was finally on the move. "I remember thinking one day in Montgomery [in 1955], 'This is what I have been preparing for my entire life,' " she said years later. " 'I don't know where it is going to take us, but we are involved in a worldwide struggle.' It was a good thing to know that my life had purpose and meaning."

The struggle Coretta King had anticipated began not much more than a year after the Kings' arrival in Montgomery. It started one December evening in 1955 when a black seamstress, Rosa Parks, refused to give up her bus seat so that a white man could sit down in comfort. Arrested, jailed, and fined, Parks became the center of an epic conflict. Black leaders instantly recognized her case as one upon which they could mount a devastating attack on segregation all over the South.

Deciding to call an all-out black boycott of the Montgomery bus system, which depended on black passengers for 75 percent of its business, the black community selected a boycott leader: the Reverend Martin Luther King, Jr. What followed was a 381-day absence of black riders, a strike that crippled the city's transportation system and ultimately forced it to integrate its buses. During that time, the Kings were subjected to a reign of terror: they received death threats, harassing telephone calls, bricks hurled through their windows. Martin Luther King was arrested and jailed, and his home was bombed.

Through it all, Coretta King stood firmly at her husband's side. "After our home in Montgomery was bombed," she said, "I had to recommit myself and my life. I realized then that I could be killed and that it was important to make this my struggle also." By now wholeheartedly dedicated to the cause her husband would die for, King saw her role as that of supporter and ally, a role she considered as important as that of frontline battler.

Repeatedly questioned about her part in the civil rights revolution, Coretta King patiently gave the same answers: "Martin's needs and the raising of our four children were my primary concern. He knew that I was going to take care of everything at home, and in this way I was able to support him and free him so that he could go and do the work of the movement."

Although she emphasized her domestic contributions, King in fact served as more than loyal helpmate. She gave speeches, participated in marches and rallies, organized concerts, and raised funds for the civil rights and peace movements. She also accompanied her husband on his world travels, acting as his ambassador and as a representative of black America. The couple's first overseas trip was to Ghana, where they helped celebrate the new nation's independence in 1957. Other King destinations included Nigeria, India, and England. In 1964 the couple traveled to Oslo, Norway, where Martin Luther King became history's youngest Nobel Peace Prize recipient.

When her husband fell to an assassin's bullet in 1968, Coretta King kept marching. Four days after his tragic death in Memphis, Tennessee, his widow led a massive rally at the site of the murder, urging Americans to seek not revenge but a "peaceful society." Two months later, Coretta King played a key role in the "Poor People's March" on Washington, D.C., making the event's keynote speech to 50,000 people.

Coretta King went on to raise her children, guard her husband's memory, and carry on his work. She founded and continues to run the Martin Luther King, Jr., Center for Nonviolent Social Change, an organization committed to achieving the slain leader's unrealized goals. In 1983, Coretta King headed the half-million people who converged on the nation's capital for the 20th anniversary of the original March on Washington. As chair of the Martin Luther King Holiday Commission, she has worked to bring all states into the annual celebration of her husband's birthday.

As she approaches the age of 70, Coretta Scott King shows no sign of flagging. She has been showered with awards and honors, including more than 100 doctoral degrees. She has been outspoken in her support for the blacks of South Africa and the leader of the African National Congress, Nelson Mandela. She continues to run the King Center, serves as cochair of the Full Employment Action Council, and maintains active memberships in the Black Leadership Roundtable and the Black Leadership Forum. She also maintains a heavy speaking schedule, addressing women's groups, children, black societies, and others on her favorite subject: the need for commitment to social justice and human rights all over the globe.

CAROL MOSELEY-BRAUN

Although her career in na-
tional politics has just begun, U.S. senator Carol
Moseley-Braun of Illinois has already had a profound
impact on the way politics is understood and con-
ducted in this country. Only the second African American to serve in the Senate since Reconstruction,
Moseley-Braun is the first black woman ever to serve
in her country's highest legislative office. Her election

on November 3, 1992, sent shock waves through an institution that has long been dominated by white males and has renewed the interest of millions of women, African Americans, and other disaffected groups in the promise of national electoral politics.

Born on August 16, 1947, in Chicago, Illinois, Carol Elizabeth Moseley was the oldest daughter of a Chicago police officer and a former hospital technician. She grew up in a segregated, middle-class neighborhood on the city's South Side, where she attended public schools along with her three younger siblings. All of the children were encouraged from an early age to prepare themselves for college and a professional career.

Even as a youngster, Moseley-Braun had little doubt concerning what her chosen profession would be—or what skills she would need to develop in order to pursue it. "I've always felt that my obligation—my calling—is to use my talents on behalf of the public interest," she recently told one reporter. "Elected officials have to be very clear that they are not leaders, but servants of the people."

After finishing high school, Moseley-Braun attended the Chicago campus of the University of Illinois, where she majored in political science. That experience deepened her desire to pursue a political career. Her next step was to return to her old neighborhood on the city's South Side, where she earned a law degree from the University of Chicago Law School.

Following law school, Moseley-Braun worked for three years as a prosecutor in the office of the U.S.

Attorney in Chicago, eventually earning that office's Special Achievement Award. It was during this period that the future politician got her first real taste of electoral politics, working as a campaign volunteer for Chicago's late mayor Harold Washington, who was then serving as a state representative. Moseley-Braun immediately fell in love with the excitement of campaigning and the challenges of public life. In 1978, with the encouragement and support of Congressman Washington and her colleagues in the U.S. Attorney's office, she ran for and was elected to a seat in the Illinois House of Representatives. She was 31 years old.

With her skills in building coalitions and her uncompromising commitment to responsible government, Moseley-Braun compiled a distinguished record during her 10 years in the Illinois state legislature, specializing in the areas of educational reform and antidiscrimination legislation. At the end of her second term, she was selected by her peers to serve as Assistant Majority Leader, making her the first African American in Illinois history to serve in that position. Though her public reputation was still modest at the time, she was already highly regarded by her fellow legislators and other groups who monitored legislative activity in the state. Incredibly, one such group, the Independent Voters of Illinois–Independent Precinct Organization (IVI–IPO), presented her with its Best Legislator Award for each of the 10 years that she served in the state House of Representatives. In 1987, Moseley-Braun was nominated by her party to run for the office of Recorder of Deeds in Cook County, a powerful but low-profile position in one of the most populous regions in the country. In a historic election, the five-term state representative accumulated more than 1 million votes to become both the first woman and the first black politician to hold an executive office in Cook County government.

Following the election, Moseley-Braun applied herself to her new job with the same vigor and tenacity with which she had performed as a legislator. She discovered soon after taking office that the county's old-fashioned, manual record-keeping system was actually costing taxpayers more money than it collected. Within months, she had replaced it with a highly efficient, computerized operation that more than doubled the state's returns by the end of the decade.

For a time, it seemed that Moseley-Braun's skills as a county executive and her commitment to her position might have taken the place of any grander political ambitions. All of that changed in September 1991, when law professor Anita Hill accused Supreme Court nominee Clarence Thomas of sexual harassment before millions of stunned television viewers.

In spite of her undeniable success in the state legislature and county government, Moseley-Braun was virtually a political unknown when she decided to give up her position as Cook County recorder of deeds and challenge fellow Democrat Alan Dixon for his seat in the U.S. Senate. A popular two-term incumbent known as Al the Pal, Dixon had angered many of his constituents in the fall by voting for Thomas's confirmation, in spite of the outspoken disapproval of the majority of women and minorities in his state.

Watching the hearings on television, Moseley-Braun was appalled at the insensitivity with which the Senate Judiciary Committee treated the real concerns of women and black people around the country. "The whole thing was an embarrassment," she would later explain. "It was an embarrassment from the beginning and by the time it got to the sexual harassment issue, it was beyond embarrassing. It was mortifying." Equally distressing was the composition of the Senate committee itself, which Moseley-Braun would later describe as "an elitist club made up of mostly White male millionaires over 50."

As the confirmation spectacle dragged on, Moseley-Braun soon discovered that she was not the only person who was outraged by what she saw. "Women were saying, 'Where are the women?'" she told one reporter. "Minorities said, 'Where are the minorities?' Workers said, 'Who are these millionaires? These aren't regular Joes.'"

With little money, few endorsements, and even less hope of actually winning her party's nomination, Moseley-Braun ran a low-key, grass-roots campaign, slowly winning support from women, blacks, and other disaffected groups throughout the state. But win or lose, her greatest goal in running was to change people's minds about who could, and should, run for national public office.

"We all thought of the Senate as this lofty place where weighty decisions were made by these serious men," she explained to one interviewer. "Instead, we saw that they were just garden variety politicians making bad speeches. We need to open up the Senate to the voices that have been excluded."

As she traveled around the state, however, and saw just how angry and disillusioned many voters had become, Moseley-Braun began to believe that she actually had a chance to win. In the final weeks of the primary, she campaigned relentlessly, overcoming a substantial lead by Dixon and the other challenger, attorney Albert Hofeld, in order to gain the Democratic nomination. Although both of her opponents had outspent her by more than 10 to 1 during the campaign, she had become the first black woman ever to win her party's nomination for the U.S. Senate.

In the general election, she faced a more formidable challenge. Her opponent in the race was Republican candidate Richard Williamson, an assistant secretary of state in the Reagan administration with years of experience in national public service. Moseley-Braun, in contrast, had no previous experience in national politics and had been able to overcome her major opponent in the primary largely on the single issue of the Thomas confirmation. Now it was the young Democratic nominee's qualifications to serve that became the issue, as Williamson and his supporters publicly attacked her inexperience in national politics and her failure to run a more substantive, issue-oriented campaign in the primary.

Moseley-Braun met the challenge, answering Williamson point by point on the issues and stubbornly defending her qualifications and experience. "This candidacy is not a fairy tale," she said to one skeptical interviewer during the campaign. "In the first place, I am qualified for this job. I am more qualified for this job than any of my opponents."

On November 3, 1992, Moseley-Braun prevailed over Williamson in a close race, gathering 53 percent of the vote and becoming the first black woman to serve in the U.S. Senate. As a freshman member of the Senate, Moseley-Braun serves on the Banking, Housing and Urban Affairs Committee; the Small Business Committee; and the powerful Judiciary Committee. Although she is now only at the beginning of her career in national politics, one of her most important goals in public life has already been realized. "To the extent that there will be other women and Black people who will see the possibilities because of my candidacy," she told a reporter during her campaign against Senator Dixon, "then I think that being nominated is a contribution that I can be proud of."

ROSA PARKS

Rosa Parks, the Birmingham seamstress who made civil rights history on a city bus in 1955, was born Rosa Louisa McCauley in Tuskegee, Alabama, on February 4, 1913. Rosa and her younger brother, Sylvester, were the children of James and Leona McCauley, a carpenter and rural schoolteacher, respectively. When Rosa was two years old,

James moved north and out of his children's life; Leona then took Rosa and Sylvester to live with her parents in Pine Level, Alabama.

Mr. and Mrs. Edwards, Rosa's grandparents, had been born into slavery, and they often talked to the little girl about the hardships and horrors of plantation life. They were kind, but both they and their daughter Leona were in poor health, which put most of the household burdens on young Rosa. She cooked and cleaned and shopped and sewed for all of them. She received a few years of tutoring from her mother, then, at the age of 11, went to stay with an aunt in Montgomery, Alabama, where she enrolled in the Montgomery Industrial School for Girls.

Too poor to pay tuition at the private institution, Rosa earned it by cleaning classrooms after school. On graduation, she entered high school, but not for long; her mother's by-now-serious illness forced the teenager to stay home and act as nurse. At 19, Rosa met and married Raymond Parks, a Montgomery barber whose greatest sorrow was his lack of education; as a young man, poverty and lack of availability had kept him out of any classroom.

Rosa Parks had been listening to the facts about racial injustice since her early childhood; Raymond's story provided one more chapter. Deeply opposed to segregation and discrimination in all their noxious forms and perhaps inspired by the experiences of her family members, she joined the National Association for the Advancement of Colored People (NAACP) in

1943. Her first NAACP assignment: to encourage local blacks to register and vote, no simple matter in the racist Deep South of the 1940s.

"As far back as I can remember," Parks said many years after reaching adulthood, "being black in Montgomery we were well aware of the inequality of our way of life. I hated it all the time. . . . My mother believed in freedom and equality even though we didn't know it for reality during our life in Alabama. . . . If a woman wanted to go in [a store] and try on a hat, they wouldn't be permitted to try it on unless they knew they were going to buy it, or they put a bag on the inside of it. In the shoe stores they had this long row of seats, and all of those in the front could be vacant, but if one of us would go in to buy, they'd always take you to the last one, to the back of the store. There were no black salespersons."

As time passed, the daily, inescapable presence of segregation grew steadily more grating to Rosa Parks. Whenever she could, she avoided public drinking fountains, movie theaters, beaches, and other facilities that flaunted WHITE and COLORED signs. If she could walk instead of riding a bus or train—with front seats off-limits to blacks—she did. Otherwise, she always faced the prospect of boarding a bus, finding a seat, then jumping up to give it to a white person when the "White" section filled up. Tired as she might be at the end of a day's work, Rosa Parks preferred walking to jumping.

Like most southern blacks, Parks had no doubt heard countless tales from friends of humiliations they suffered on the Montgomery transit system. One woman recalled that when she and her blind husband boarded a bus too slowly to suit the driver, he shut the door on the man's leg, then stepped on the gas. Another black passenger told of getting on a bus without the exact change and, when he hesitated, being chased off at gunpoint by the driver. A third man spoke of his pregnant wife, forced by a driver to give up her seat to a young white woman, and yet another recalled a driver calling her an "ugly black ape."

Understandably, when Parks had the energy, she walked home from work. By the 1950s, she was holding a reasonably good job. She had always enjoyed sewing, and now she worked at Montgomery Fair, a city department store, doing alterations for customers. The job was pleasant enough, but Parks spent most of the long workday on her feet.

One late fall day—it was Thursday, December 1, 1955—the 42-year-old Parks finished her work, boarded a Cleveland Avenue bus, and sank into a seat. "Coming up to the Christmas holiday," she said later, "the work was a bit heavy. When I left the store that evening I was tired." Parks sat next to a black man in the first row of the back section, which was traditionally reserved for blacks. The first 10 rows of the bus—always off-limits to blacks—were filled with white passengers.

A few stops after Parks had taken her seat, a white man boarded the bus and looked around for a place to sit. This was the signal, of course, for a "good nigra"—a white southerner's phrase for a humble, deferential black person—to give the white passenger his or her seat, then go to the back of the bus and stand. But on this day, there seemed to be a shortage of good nigras. No one moved.

Sighing with exasperation, the driver stopped the bus, walked back to Parks and her seatmate, and said, "Y'all make it light on yourselves and let me have those seats." The black man rose and moved to the back. Parks stayed put. The driver seemed to be trying to keep his voice under control. "If you don't stand up," he told Parks, "I'm going to call the police and have you arrested." By now, Parks had moved too many times, had stood aside too many times, had waited for service too many times. Tense but absolutely determined, she looked straight at the furious driver. "You may do that," she said softly.

Writing of that moment, civil rights activist Eldridge Cleaver said, "Somewhere in the universe a gear in the machinery had shifted."

Called by the bus driver, two policemen boarded at the next stop and said to Parks: "Why don't you stand up?" "I don't think I should have to," she replied. The officers arrested Parks, booked her on a misdemeanor charge, and released her on a $100 bond. The news flashed through the black community, whose members had long been considering some action against the bus company, its arrogant drivers, and segregation in general. Black leaders asked if they could use her case as a test case, and after conferring with her mother and her husband, she agreed. "I just felt resigned to give what I could to protest," she said.

When Parks's case came up for trial a few days later, she was found guilty and fined $10 plus $4 in court costs. She refused to pay and filed an appeal. Now the gears began to move. Inspired by a young Montgomery clergyman named Martin Luther King, Jr., blacks organized a one-day boycott of the city's buses. Its success led to a 381-day strike by the black community, 25,000 people who accounted for 75 percent of the bus company's business.

Meanwhile, the department store fired Rosa Parks; her husband lost his job as well. Parks began to receive threatening telephone calls and letters; she responded by helping to arrange car pools so that people could get to work without riding the buses. At last, on June 2, 1956, the U.S. District Court ruled that segregated seating on buses was unconstitutional; the ruling was upheld by the U.S. Supreme Court, which, in December 1956, ordered Montgomery to integrate its buses. Rosa Parks's gesture of defiance had sparked the civil rights movement of the 1950s and 1960s, tumultuous decades that would change the course of American social history forever.

Unable to find other jobs in the wake of publicity surrounding the boycott, Parks, her husband, and her mother moved to Detroit in 1957. Parks worked as a seamstress for several years, spending her free time volunteering at the Detroit branch of the Southern Christian Leadership Conference (SCLC). In 1965, U.S. congressman John Conyers of Detroit hired her as his staff assistant, a job she held until her retirement in 1988. In 1992, she published *Rosa Parks: My*

Story, an autobiography written with the aid of Jim Haskins. Rosa Parks received the NAACP's coveted Spingarn Medal in 1979 and the Martin Luther King, Jr., Nonviolent Peace Prize in 1980. She has been awarded numerous other awards and honors and holds ten honorary college degrees. Upon reaching her 80th birthday in 1993, Parks said she planned to continue to fight injustice. "I have no choice but to keep on," she said.

MADAM C. J. WALKER

$\mathbf{M}$adam C. J. Walker, America's first black female millionaire, was born Sarah Breedlove on December 23, 1867. She spent her poverty-stricken early years on the Delta, Louisiana, cotton plantation where her parents had worked as field slaves. By the time she was five, Sarah herself was planting seed and hauling water to the sharecroppers.

Owen and Minerva Breedlove dreamed of educating Sarah and her two siblings, but the dream proved elusive. Their former masters had never taught them to read or write, and in the virulent racism of the postwar Deep South, schools for black children were almost nonexistent. Sarah reached adulthood illiterate.

In 1874, yellow fever swept through the Delta area; among its victims were Owen and Minerva Breedlove. Unable to support themselves in Delta, Sarah and her older sister, Louvenia, traveled to Vicksburg, Mississippi, where they found work as laundresses.

In 1882, 14-year-old Sarah married Moses McWilliams, a Vicksburg laborer. Three years later, she gave birth to a daughter, whom she and her husband happily named Lelia. But soon after the child's second birthday, McWilliams died in an accident, leaving young Sarah an impoverished single mother.

Told that St. Louis offered more opportunity, Sarah McWilliams bought a boat ticket, put Lelia on her hip, and headed up the Mississippi. She found work as a laundress and soon started Lelia in school, a move that gave her profound satisfaction. Nevertheless, she constantly dreamed of a finer life for her daughter and herself. "But with all my thinking," she said years later, "I couldn't see how I, a poor washerwoman, was going to better my condition."

McWilliams worked and saved and did without all but the bare necessities, and when Lelia graduated from high school, she was able to send her to a small black college in Knoxville, Tennessee. To help pay the tuition, McWilliams started selling hair products from door to door. Like many other black women, she had conformed to fashion by trying to straighten her hair; as a result it was now broken and patchy and revealed her scalp in several places.

Realizing that the product she was peddling did nothing for her hair, McWilliams decided to develop her own. The formula, she said later, came to her in a dream. "In that dream," she recalled, "a big black man appeared to me and told me what to mix up for my hair. Some of it was grown in Africa, but I sent for it, mixed it, put it on my scalp, and in a few weeks, my hair was coming in faster than it had ever fallen out. . . . I made up my mind to begin to sell it."

The 38-year-old McWilliams now decided to change her surroundings and go into business. On July 21, 1905, she arrived in Denver, Colorado, with her hair formula and her life savings: $1.50. She rented an attic room, joined a church, found a job as a cook, and began making small batches of the new potions she had devised: Wonderful Hair Grower, Glossine, and Vegetable Shampoo. Door-to-door sales proved successful; other black women bought Walker's goods as fast as she could make them.

In early 1906, McWilliams married C. J. Walker, a newspaperman with experience in advertising and direct-mail selling. Whites of the era automatically called blacks by their first names: to avoid that irritant, the entrepreneur now called herself Madam C. J. Walker, which also lent an exotic touch to her products. With her husband's help, Walker turned her small business into an industry. The pair developed major differences, however, first about the business, then about personal matters. They divorced in 1912, but Sarah Walker retained her married name.

Meanwhile, A'Lelia Walker Robinson (who had graduated from college, married, divorced, and added an *A* to her first name) had become her mother's right hand. A'Lelia oversaw the moves of the Walker Company, first from Denver to Pittsburgh, then from Pittsburgh to Indianapolis. In 1915, at her daughter's urging, Walker moved to New York City, although she kept her manufacturing base in Indianapolis.

By this point, Sarah Breedlove Walker had become a wealthy woman, well known both for her business success and her extraordinary contributions to black schools, housing projects, old people's homes, orphanages, and civil rights groups. She had hired a nucleus of highly educated aides—attorneys, teachers, accountants, and other professionals—and had learned not only to read and write but to appreciate literature, classical music, art, architecture, and the theater.

After Walker's move to an elegant town house in New York's Harlem, she bought a tract of land in the New York suburb of Irvington-on-Hudson, hired a prominent black architect, and built a mansion. Called the Villa Lewaro (for LElia WAlker RObinson), the huge and stately residence awed even Walker's wealthy white neighbors. At first, some complained. "The villagers, noting her color, were frankly puzzled," reported the *New York Times*. "When it became known that she was the owner [of the mansion], they could only gasp in astonishment. 'Impossible!' they exclaimed. 'No woman of her race could own such a place.'" But she could, and she did. Soon after she settled into Villa Lewaro, her affluent neighbors came to regard her with respect.

Walker's acceptance by her white neighbors pleased her; even more pleasing was her acceptance by black leaders. In 1912, she had addressed the National Negro Business League's annual convention, but only after the frosty disapproval of its president: the great Booker T. Washington showed notoriously little regard for female entrepreneurs. But Walker's star rose so quickly that Washington soon changed his tune; introducing her as keynote speaker at the league's 1913 convention, he called her "one of the most progressive and successful" blacks in American business.

Walker had not only made herself a millionaire; she had also created prosperous lives for the thousands of black women she employed as agents. As the company expanded from its attic-workshop stage in Denver, it steadily enlarged both its product line and its sales force. Leading that force was Walker herself, who traveled almost constantly, making speeches, opening new Walker beauty salons and "colleges" for training operators, and signing up saleswomen.

By 1919, some 25,000 people, almost all of them black and female, sold Walker products. Their enthusiasm seems to have been deep and genuine—as well it might have been, considering the enormous difference a Walker job could make in a woman's life.

At the time, a black woman worker averaged $10 per week in the North and $2 per week in the South. A typical Walker agent or "hair culturist" (beautician) made $23 per week.

"I have all I can do at home and don't have to go out and work for white people in kitchens and factories," wrote one enthusiastic operator to Walker. Another wrote: "You have opened up a trade for hundreds of colored women to make an honest and profitable living where they make as much in one week as a month's salary would bring from any other position that a colored woman can secure."

Concerned about her escalating blood pressure, Walker's doctors constantly begged her to slow down, but she would not or could not. During World War I, for example, she had visited dozens of military bases, talking to black soldiers about their role in the war and the future; in 1917, she had helped organize and participated in the Negro Silent Protest Parade, a massive demonstration against racial violence.

Almost to the end of her life, Walker traveled thousands of miles a year, made dozens of speeches, and oversaw almost every facet of her sprawling empire. But in 1919, her erratic heart finally forced her to rest. Aware that her time was growing short, she made a list of bequests, establishing a $200,000 trust fund to go to "worthy charities" and leaving sums ranging from $2,000 to $5,000 to such institutions as the Colored Orphans Home in St. Louis, the Home for Aged and Infirm Colored People in Pittsburgh, the Haines Institute in Georgia, the National Association for the

Advancement of Colored People, and Tuskegee Institute. That done, she looked up at her nurse and murmured, "I want to live to help my race." Soon afterward, Sarah Breedlove Walker died at the age of 51.

America's first black self-made female millionaire, Walker never forgot her roots. A child of poverty, she eagerly shared her immense wealth with the needy. Deprived of an early education, she made a point of supporting schools. Born to former slaves, she vigorously exercised her rights as an American citizen, using her economic and personal power to strengthen her community and urging others to follow her lead.

Wherever she spoke, Walker encouraged black women and men to pursue their dreams. "I promoted myself," she often told her audiences. "I had to make my own living and my own opportunity! But I made it! Don't sit down and wait for the opportunities to come. Get up and make them!"

IDA B. WELLS-BARNETT

Ida B. Wells-Barnett, jour-
nalist and antilynching activist, was born Ida Bell
Wells on July 16, 1862, in Holly Springs, Mississippi.
A slave at birth, she—along with her family and the
rest of the Confederacy's blacks—became legally free
when President Abraham Lincoln signed the Eman-
cipation Proclamation on January 1, 1863. Ida was the
first of the eight children born to Jim Wells, son of a

white master and a slave mother, and Elizabeth War-renton Wells.

In the immediate postwar years, the Wells family prospered: Jim's independent carpentry shop did well, and his wife and older children attended Shaw University, a Holly Springs school opened by the Freedmen's Aid Society. Then, in 1876, tragedy struck: a yellow fever epidemic blasted through Tennessee and Mississippi, taking hundreds of victims, among them Jim and Elizabeth Wells and their youngest child.

A shocked 14-year-old Ida now found herself in charge of the family. To support her siblings, she took a job teaching at a country school for blacks, later moving with her two youngest sisters to Memphis, Tennessee. There she found another country-school position and took advanced courses at the city's black college, LeMoyne Institute.

Boarding the train to work one day in May 1884, the 21-year-old Wells seated herself in her usual car, the first-class ladies' coach. A new conductor took her ticket, then demanded that she move to the smoking car, the only one appropriate, he said, for blacks. Wells refused; she had paid for a first-class coach, and that was where she would ride. When two burly guards tried to force her into the smoking car, she left the train, then hired a lawyer and sued the railroad. To the consternation of some local whites, she won; a Minnesota-born judge ordered the Chesapeake and Ohio Railroad to pay her $500. The *Memphis Appeal* reported the news in a headline: DARKY DAMSEL GETS DAMAGES.

Wells's elation in her vindication proved short-lived; the railroad appealed, and the Tennessee Supreme Court reversed the earlier decision. For "colored people," said the court, the smoking car *was* the first-class coach. It ordered Wells to pay $200 in court costs. From that point on, Ida Wells would dedicate herself to the cause of equality and justice for her race.

For the next seven years, Wells continued to teach in the winter and study in the summer. For entertainment, she went to musical evenings and literary-club meetings. At these gatherings, members read aloud from such publications as the literary *Evening Star*, which Wells had begun to edit, the local weekly, *Living Way*, and the *Free Speech and Headlight*, a militantly pro–civil rights newspaper. Impressed with her work in the *Star*, the editor of the *Living Way* asked Wells to write for his paper.

Wells's fiery *Living Way* articles—signed "Iola"—soon attracted the attention of the black intellectual community. The pieces were hard to ignore, containing such lines as: "A Winchester rifle should have a place of honor in every black home, and it should be used for that protection which the law refuses to give." Other black publications, such as the *New York Age*, the *Indianapolis Freeman*, and the *Little Rock Sun*, began to reprint and comment on "Iola's" stories about black life in Tennessee.

In 1889 the owner of *Free Speech and Headlight* offered Wells the editorship of his small but influential paper. She accepted, soon almost doubling the journal's circulation and filling its pages with tough rhetoric about race relations. Under Wells's leadership, the paper earned a reputation for speaking out against injustice, no matter what its source.

In 1891, Wells, who continued to teach full-time, published a highly critical article about the Memphis Board of Education and its short-changing of the city's black schools. The article aimed at reform; instead, it got its author fired from teaching. Wells's next brush with the city's white establishment came a year later. It began when a crowd of whites raided a jail where three black men—all of them friends of Wells's—were being held on trumped-up charges of inciting to riot. The mob dragged the blacks to the outskirts of town and shot them dead.

Responding to the lynching with a burst of fury on her front page, Wells advised the city's blacks to move away from Memphis, which she described as "a town which will neither protect our lives and property, nor give us a fair trial in the courts, but take us out and murder us in cold blood when accused by a white person." Two thousand blacks took her advice, almost crippling Memphis's streetcar company and infuriating whites. Two months later, Wells wrote another editorial, this one provoked by another lynching.

Observing that most lynchings took place to punish black men for raping white women, she implied that many such alleged rapes were no such thing. Instead, she suggested, they were voluntary relationships between people who found each other sexually attractive. This was more than the white male South could tolerate. Mobs burned and looted the offices and presses of the *Free Speech*, and other newspapers ran open threats against Wells, warning her to leave Memphis if she wished to live.

Wells moved to New York City and became a columnist for the *New York Age*, a crusading newspaper owned by black press titan T. Thomas Fortune. Wells started her association with the newspaper by writing a long, frank, and deeply thoughtful article about lynching and its history. The piece, later published in a pamphlet as *Southern Horrors*, drew a tremendous response from the nation's black community. Fortune printed and sold tens of thousands of reprints; even Frederick Douglass took note. Making a special visit to New York, the great abolitionist thanked Wells for setting the record straight on lynching.

Next, Wells began a lecture tour, explaining southern lynching to audiences in the Northeast. Attending one of her speeches in 1893 was Catherine Impey, an Englishwoman who had been fighting discrimination in Britain for years. Impey, impressed with Wells and her message, invited the Memphis exile to repeat her lecture tour in England, Scotland, and Wales.

Britons listened to Wells with sympathetic rage; she listened to them with curiosity. Particularly impressive to the American woman were the civic associations of her British counterparts. In organized groups, she realized, lay strength. On her return to America in May 1893, she began advising American women to do as British women did—advice that would give a strong push to the black women's club movement, eventually a powerful force for change.

Thanks in large measure to Wells, several influential organizations came into being during the next few years: the National Conference of Colored Women, the National Federation of Afro-American Women, the National League of Colored Women. Behind these umbrella groups were countless smaller clubs at church, school, and community levels, many of them also inspired by Wells's speeches.

In 1893, Wells moved to Chicago, which would be her home base for the rest of her life. She took a job with the *Chicago Conservator*, a black newspaper founded by lawyer Ferdinand L. Barnett, and started Chicago's first civic club for black women. Like similar organizations Wells had sparked, this one concentrated on publicizing and trying to halt lynching. In 1894, she returned to England for another round of lectures about lynching; the following year, she married Barnett, a man whose goals and dreams matched her own. For professional reasons, she took the then-unusual step of using both her husband's and her own family name.

At first, Ida B. Wells-Barnett considered leaving public life, but its lure and her sense of duty soon brought her back to the crusade for justice. She would bear four children and maintain a happy marriage, but she would also keep on writing articles, making speeches, attending conferences, reporting on racial violence, and helping to found activist clubs. In 1898, she led a delegation to President William McKinley to protest lynching; in the same year, she became secretary of the National Afro-American Council. In 1908, she founded the Negro Fellowship League; in 1913, she was appointed as a Chicago adult probation officer. Also in 1913, she founded the first black woman suffrage organization, the Alpha Suffrage Club of Chicago. In 1915, she was elected vice-president of Chicago's Equal Rights League. Wells-Barnett remained active until a sudden attack of uremic poisoning sent her to the hospital in 1931. She died two days later.

Writing in the *Crisis* newspaper, author, editor, and educator W. E. B. Du Bois said, "Ida Wells-Barnett was the pioneer of the anti-lynching crusade. She began the awakening of the conscience of the nation."

❧ FURTHER READING ☙

Shirley Chisholm

Chisholm, Shirley. *The Good Fight.* New York: Harper and Row, 1973.

————. *Unbought and Unbossed.* New York: Houghton Mifflin, 1970.

Scheader, Catherine. *Shirley Chisholm: Teacher and Congresswoman.* Hillside, NJ: Enslow, 1990.

Marian Wright Edelman

Edelman, Marian Wright. *The Measure of Our Success: A Letter to My Children and Yours.* Boston: Beacon Press, 1992.

Tomkins, Calvin. "Profiles: A Sense of Urgency." *New Yorker*, March 1989, 48–74.

Barbara Jordan

Blue, Rose, and Corinne Naden. *Barbara Jordan.* New York: Chelsea House, 1992.

Haskins, James. *Barbara Jordan.* New York: Dial Press, 1977.

Jordan, Barbara, and Shelby Hearon. *Barbara Jordan: A Self-Portrait.* New York: Doubleday, 1979.

Coretta Scott King

Garrow, David J. *Bearing the Cross: Martin Luther King, Jr., and the Southern Christian Leadership Conference.* New York: Morrow, 1986.

King, Coretta Scott. *My Life with Martin Luther King, Jr.* New York: Holt, 1969.

Carol Moseley-Braun

"Braun Pauses for Thanks After a Rocky Campaign." *USA Today*, November 4, 1992, A8.

Clay, William L. *Just Permanent Interests: Black Americans in Congress, 1870–1991.* New York: Penguin, 1992.

Haynes, Karima A. "Will Carol Moseley Braun Be the First Black Woman Senator?" *Ebony*, June 1992, 120–22.

Ragsdale, Bruce, and Joel D. Treese, eds. *Black Americans in Congress, 1870–1989.* Washington, D.C.: Government Printing Office, 1990.

Wilkerson, Isabel. "Storming Senate 'Club': Carol Elizabeth Moseley Braun." *New York Times*, March 19, 1992, A20.

Rosa Parks

Branch, Taylor. *Parting the Waters: America in the King Years 1954–1963.* New York: Simon and Schuster, 1988.

Parks, Rosa, with Jim Haskins. *Rosa Parks: My Story.* New York: Dial Books, 1992.

Robinson, Jo Ann. *The Montgomery Bus Boycott and the Women Who Started It.* Nashville: University of Tennessee Press, 1987.

Madam C. J. Walker

Bundles, A'Lelia Perry. *Madam C. J. Walker.* New York: Chelsea House, 1991.

Ida B. Wells-Barnett

Neverdon-Morton, Cynthia. *Afro-American Women of the South and the Advancement of Race, 1895–1925.* Nashville: University of Tennessee Press, 1989.

❦ INDEX ❧

❦ Picture Credits ❧

RICHARD RENNERT has edited the nearly 100 volumes in Chelsea House's award-winning BLACK AMERICANS OF ACHIEVEMENT series, which tells the stories of black men and women who have helped shape the course of modern history. He is also the author of several sports biographies, including *Henry Aaron*, *Jesse Owens*, and *Jackie Robinson*. He is a graduate of Haverford College in Haverford, Pennsylvania.